Prospecting for Benefactors

Books by Mathew Iredale

The Problem of Free Will, a contemporary introduction
Prospecting for Benefactors: How to find major donors to support your school

Prospecting for Benefactors

How to find major donors to support *your* school

MATHEW IREDALE

Copyright © 2015 Mathew Iredale

The moral rights of the author have been asserted.

All rights reserved. No part of this publication may be reproduced, distributed, or transmitted in any form or by any means, including photocopying, recording, or other electronic or mechanical methods, without the prior written permission of the publisher, except in the case of brief quotations embodied in critical reviews and certain other non-commercial uses permitted by copyright law.

All enquiries to mail@fundraisingresearch.info

British Library Cataloguing-in-Publication Data
A catalogue record for this book is available from the British Library.

ISBN-10: 1497509157
ISBN-13: 978-1497509153

Designed and typeset in Garamond.

*Give a man a fish
and you feed him for a day.*

*Teach a man to fish
and you feed him for life.*

Contents

1 Introduction
    1.1 A practical guide   1
    1.2 Prospect research   2
    1.3 Estimating wealth   3

2 Identifying prospects through your school community
    2.1 Getting started   7
    2.2 Staff   9
    2.3 Parents   10
    2.4 Alumni   10

3 Identifying prospects through your database
    3.1 The power of the database   13
    3.2 Past donors   14
    3.3 Private banks   17
    3.4 Occupation   19
    3.5 Email addresses   20
    3.6 Property   21
    3.7 Tax havens   24
    3.8 Titled people   24
    3.9 Wealth screening   25

4 Identifying prospects through other sources
    4.1 Paying school fees in advance   29
    4.2 Biographies   30
    4.3 LinkedIn & Facebook   31
    4.4 Newspapers   35
    4.5 Local businessmen and women   36

5 Qualifying Prospects
    5.1 Qualification as triage   39
    5.2 Check your database   41
    5.3 Property value   42
    5.4 Companies House   44
    5.5 Who's Who & People of Today   48
    5.6 LinkedIn   50
    5.7 Trustees of charitable trusts   51
    5.8 Other philanthropy   52

5.9 News archives	54
5.10 Practise makes perfect	55
5.11 Troubleshooting	59
6 Ranking Prospects	
6.1 The gift pyramid	63
6.2 Gift capacity	65
6.3 Warmth and affinity	67
6.4 Conclusion	70

Appendix A – Prospect spreadsheet
Appendix B – Private bank accounts
Appendix C – Qualification flow chart
Appendix D – Ranked prospect list

Acknowledgements

1

Introduction

1.1 A practical guide

The purpose of this book is to enable you – to empower you - to find people who are capable of supporting your fundraising appeal with a major gift.

What is a major gift? This really depends upon the size of your appeal, but generally speaking, a major gift is any donation that makes a significant difference. For some appeals this will be a gift of £25,000 or more, for others it will be a gift of £500 or less. Either way, the principals involved in identifying prospective major donors, or prospects, are the same.

My motivation in writing this book is very simple. There are a great many books about major gift fundraising, and how to run a capital campaign, but they all share the same basic shortcomings. Firstly, they generally devote one chapter to identifying potential major donors when this is a subject to which one can devote a whole book (you're holding it in your hand right now) and secondly, the advice they provide is invariably long on theory and short on the practical steps you actually need to take.

This book is different.

It offers tried and tested techniques from someone who has been finding major gift prospects for schools, hospitals and charities for many years and who appreciates the problems you will face when trying to identify them and who knows the solutions. In this book I will show you how to find wealthy people who are willing and able to support *your* school with a major gift.

It is particularly aimed at those who have little or no experience of finding prospects. If you are launching a fundraising campaign for the first time or you have been there before but wish for a little helping hand, a little confidence giver, then this is the book for you.

1.2 Prospect research

To find major gift prospects you need to employ a technique (really, a set of techniques requiring various skills) called prospect research. Prospect research involves identifying and then researching major gift prospects and is the first and vital step in Major Gift fundraising, the process by which you secure significant gifts from your prospects. Classically, it involves the following stages:

1. **Identification** – the stage at which you identify major gift prospects from amongst the larger school community of alumni, parents, former parents, etc.

2. **Qualification** – the method by which you sort the suitable prospects from the unsuitable, ranking those who remain, so that you know who to approach first and for what level of donation.

3. **Cultivation** – the stage during which you approach the prospect and try to interest them in your school and its fundraising appeal.

4. **Solicitation** – the critical stage at which you ask the prospect for a donation, or to pledge a donation, and – most importantly – thank them for their support!

5. **Stewardship** – this is the stage during which you recognise the donor's support in an appropriate way (usually through naming opportunities), and continue to cultivate and strengthen your relationship with them, in appreciation of what they have done and in the hope that one day they will wish to support you again.

In this book, I will take you step by step through the first two stages: identification and qualification. By the end you will be in possession of a list of prospects ready to be cultivated for a major gift in support of your fundraising appeal.

In the first three chapters you will learn about the various techniques I have used over the years for identifying prospects. Chapter 4 takes you through the research resources you will need to qualify the prospects you find to create a pool of the best prospects to cultivate. In Chapter 5, I discuss how to rank these prospects, so that you know who in your prospect pool to solicit first for a major gift and who to leave until later.

1.3 Estimating wealth

So far so good. But now the bad news. It is possible to accurately estimate wealth *for very few people indeed*. To be really accurate you need publicly available information (ownership of land, property, obvious assets such as art or shares in publicly quoted companies). For the rest, you have to guess. In 2005, Philip Beresford (the man who compiles The Sunday Times Rich List) estimated that of the 500 people or families worth £100m or more listed in the Rich List, there were another 500 who could not be included because there was little or no publicly available information about their wealth.

But luckily for us, we don't need to be able to find hard evidence of someone's wealth. All we need to do is to find enough circumstantial evidence such that it is (much) more likely than not that the person is capable of a major gift. Unlike Philip Beresford, we do not need to compile an accurate rich list, able to withstand close scrutiny by financial experts and the public alike. All we need to do is to identify those people from amongst our alumni and parents who are *most likely* to have money. All we need to do is to identify certain wealth *indicators*. The more you identify, the more likely it is that your prospect is capable of making a major gift. This method is not error-proof – there will always be those who slip through your net – but for those prospects for whom there is no publicly available information regarding their wealth, wealth indicators are the tried and tested method of identifying your best prospects.

In chapter 2, I will show you how you can use wealth indicators to identify your best prospects, but before then it is time for *you* to have a think about who may be a potential major donor in your school community.

Prospecting for Benefactors

2

Identifying prospects through your school community

2.1 Getting started

When starting on a major gift fundraising appeal, one of the first things you should do is to sit down with a pen and paper and write a list of everyone connected with your school who you think may be wealthy or, just as importantly, know someone who is wealthy.

If you need a bit of help to get you going, then start with the names of your governors and Head. I don't care if they don't have any money; they will know people. All governors do. Then think about parents (do you have a parents association? If so, who sits on it?) and alumni (do you have an alumni committee? Who sits on that?) Write down these names and any others who come to mind. Anyone, in fact, who is remotely connected to your school and who you think may be wealthy or who knows someone who is wealthy.

This is your primary list, containing all the key people connected to your school. Or most of them, anyway. The idea here is very simple. You need to find people to either ask for a major gift or at least be able to introduce you to the person who is going to do the asking (whether it is the Head, your chair of governors, the development director, or someone else). In creating your primary list, you should only (or mostly) think of those people who fit the categories above (having wealth or knowing someone with wealth).

Hopefully, you will be able to think of a good few names. If you are very unlucky, you may have ground to a halt after the governors and the Head. Don't worry if you have; finding more names is what this book is for, after all.

The next step is to ask your governors and Senior Leadership Team to do the same – to create a list of wealthy people (or those with good networks) within the school community *who they know personally*. You may think, 'why would someone want to support my school if they have no connection to it?' It may seem unlikely, but it does happen. Admittedly most people who are unconnected with a school will not support it, but occasionally – for the right appeal and if asked by the right person – they will. It's always useful to bear such people in mind, just in case. If a governor is at all reluctant to give you a name, even if you know full well that they know the person, do not press the matter. At this stage it is important to have the governors onside and unnecessary badgering will only be counter-productive. There is plenty of time for governors (and others) to warm to the idea that they can suggest friends and peers as prospects without having to sell their soul to the devil.

Collate the names (keeping a note of who named who) and then put the list to one side. As you begin to identify prospects, you need to keep the primary list to hand to see if any of their names come up and how many times. These people will be amongst the first you will want to approach for support because they are known to people in leadership roles in your school.

I also recommend you create a Prospect spreadsheet in Excel, to list all the prospects you will identify through the various techniques I discuss in the following chapters (see Appendix A for an example of this spreadsheet).

2.2 Staff

Teaching Staff – especially senior staff, house masters & mistresses and form teachers – can be a valuable source for identifying prospects, having first-hand knowledge of both alumni and parents. And do not forget retired teachers.

Teachers can provide valuable information as to what an alumnus was like when they were a pupil (sporty, academic, their hobbies and interests) and possibly also what they are up to now, if they have kept in contact.

And although many schools now record parental information as standard (e.g. job title, profession, email address) there is certain information – how the parents really feel about the school, who flashes the cash or who is struggling financially – that will not be recorded, but of which the teaching staff could well be aware. How should you record such potentially delicate information? With tact, is my suggestion.

For this reason, it is worth setting up 121 meetings with appropriate members of staff. You can either ask them to suggest alumni or parents who they think fit your criteria, or you could take along the primary list to get the discussion going. And do reassure them that when contact is made with an alumnus, they will not be named as the source.

2.3 Parents

Many of the points about staff also apply to parents. Parents talk to each other and, as with the teaching staff, know how other parents feel about the school, who has money and who does not.

The most obvious place to start is with your Parents Association, and any parents you know personally, and then work out from there, based on their recommendations. Again, if necessary, do reassure them about anonymity when approaching anyone they suggest.

2.4 Alumni

Your alumni association is another valuable source for identifying prospects. Many alumni keep in touch with each other and meet others at events and so can have a very good idea of who is doing well. Start with your alumni committee and work out from there. As before, reassure them about anonymity.

In the next two chapters I discuss various techniques for identifying prospects through your database and beyond, but I wish to emphasise that you can only find out so much through databases and websites; as we have seen in this chapter, there are other ways of identifying prospects and you must use them.

Prospecting for Benefactors

3

Identifying prospects through your database

3.1 The power of the database

If you want to identify major gift prospects then one of the most obvious places to start looking is your database of alumni and parents.

If you don't have a database then you must create one.

In this day and age you cannot undertake effective fundraising without one. If you have a list of alumni and parents on a spreadsheet, then you may be able to upload the relevant information into a database without too much hassle (or hire someone who can do it for you). If you only have people listed on card index, papyrus or vellum, then you'll have to input the information by hand.

If you don't have a list of any alumni at all then you could do worse than log onto LinkedIn and create a group for your school, if one does not exist already. Then search for people who went to your school and invite them to join your group. I discuss the best way to do this in section 4.3 (page 31).

Until then, you can skip forward to Chapter 4, but I do urge you to create a database of alumni and parents as soon as you can.

3.2 Past donors

If there is absolutely no history of fundraising at your school, or no gifts listed on your database, then you may wish to skip this first section.

Unless you already have a very good idea of the history of giving to your school then I strongly recommend, before anything else, <u>searching your database for all past donors</u>. Not only will this give you an idea of the level of previous philanthropic support for your school – always useful to know before launching a fundraising appeal – it may also throw up a number of prospects; if someone has previously given you a donation, especially a sizeable one, they may be prepared to do so again.

As they say with shares, past performance is no guarantee of future performance, but even so, knowing that a prospect has given you £20,000 in the past is a very good guide to their being able to do so again. You do get one-off donations, especially to capital appeals for one's old school. But unless their circumstances have changed in any significant way since their donation, knowing what someone has given in the past is one of the best indicators of what they can give now.

At what level should your search for past donors start? That is really up to you, as schools differ widely in the level of philanthropic support they have received in the past. If you really have no idea, then start by searching for donors of £500 or more and if this results in a list of more than 50 people, you should raise the amount to £1,000 and try again. If, on the other hand, you get no results, then lower the amount to £100, say, and try again. If your search brings up little or nothing then do not get disheartened – this is what this book is for; to find people who *will* support your school.

How far back should your search go? As far back as your database goes, certainly, and even further if you have the time and inclination to search through your school archives and accounts. When I worked at Great Ormond Street Hospital (admittedly not a school, but there are similarities) I decided to compile a list of all significant donors to the hospital from its foundation in 1852 to the present day. By significant, I was looking for anyone who was well known or notable in some way: celebrities, politicians, that sort of thing. Obviously, there were no databases in the 'good old days' of Charles Dickens (who was one of the hospital's first significant donors) and so a considerable amount of old-fashioned research was required, by which I mean I could not simply turn on a computer and search the internet.

I read books and articles on the history of the hospital, waded through various newspaper cuttings and other archive material in the hospital museum, and sifted through reams of faded computer printouts kept by the Finance Department from the days of the Wishing Well

Appeal of the 1980s. Some very interesting names came up, including several forebears of living wealthy individuals.

Which brings me to an important point: some of your past major donors may be deceased (if you have a long history of philanthropy, many of them will be) but this is no reason to discard them. Their children, grandchildren, or other relatives, may have attended your school. If so, you should add *them* to your list of prospects.

For many schools, such extensive archived material is not available, but unless you look for it, you won't know what useful information *is* to be found in past school annual reports, alumni newsletters and school magazines, or who you may uncover.

One-off donations above a certain level are only one sign of wealth. Another sign is a series of donations, spread over a year, or two years, or five years, that add up to a significant amount. If a donor has given donations of between £50 and £100 every few months for several years, the first search of donations of £500 or more will not pick them up. Nevertheless, their donations may add up to several thousand pounds over the years, indicating they may be wealthy and worth marking as a prospect.

Once you have imported the list of previous donors into your Prospect spreadsheet you need to order them by donation size and date, to identify the largest, most recent donors.

3.3 Private banks

Identifying alumni and parents who use a private bank account is possibly the best technique to identify prospects in your database. Private Banks offer specialist services (wealth management, tax advice, loans for yachts) for those with a significant level of wealth and as such, they generally require their clients to have, at least, several hundred thousand pounds with which to open an account. There is no guarantee that someone with a private bank account is wealthy, but it is much more likely than not.

If you look at the table in Appendix B you will see the level of wealth generally required to open an account with a private bank (based on the bank's own website, news archives and banking and finance websites).

There are two ways to identify alumni with a private bank account. The first is to look out for donations received or fees paid using a private bank cheque. Ask your Gift Manager, Finance Manager, or whoever it is that banks the cheques, to look out for any cheques that are not from one of the high street banks. They often have quite distinctive designs and so are easy to spot.

The second way is to search for private bank accounts already listed in your database. The easiest way to do this is to export the whole list of bank names (with the name of the account holder) into a password protected spreadsheet, sort them alphabetically, and delete the high street banks from the list. You do not need individual bank account details for this search and so *on no account* should you export such confidential information to your spreadsheet.

I have heard it said that searching a database for people with private bank accounts violates the Data Protection Act. I just wish to stress that this is not true. I have personally checked with the Information Commissioners Office (who are responsible for the enforcement of the Act) and they have confirmed that searching a database for private bank account holders does not violate the Act.

But there are two important caveats to this. The first is that the person has voluntarily given you his bank account details to enable you to carry out a legitimate task (e.g. to process a donation or pay for school fees). The second is that the person has read and agreed to your data protection policy, and that it specifically states that you may use the information they give you for fundraising. Many schools already include such a sentence in their data protection policy (e.g. "The School will, from time to time, make use of personal data relating to students, parents or guardians for fundraising purposes."). Do check that your school is one of them. If not, make sure that a suitable sentence is added and that you make this change known to the alumni and parent body.

Finally – it is stating the obvious, but – do please remember that a person's bank account details are *confidential*, and rightly so. It is absolutely vital that you maintain confidentiality when compiling a list of prospects using private bank account details.

When you have completed your search, import the list of private bank account holders into your Prospect spreadsheet and order them by amount of assets required, with the largest at the top.

3.4 Occupation

The next technique to identify prospects on your database is to search by occupation/job title. Knowing someone's profession and seniority can tell you a great deal about their wealth (and networks).

Anyone with a senior job title such as Chief Executive, Chairman, Managing Director, Partner, Managing Partner, President, Vice President or Founder, is worth flagging up as a prospect.

There are also various finance-related job titles that are worth looking for. E.g. Accountant, Fund Manager, Hedge Fund Manager, Financier, Banker, Investment Banker, Merchant Banker, Private Banker, Investment Analyst, Equity Analyst, Equity Trader, Investment Manager, Stockbroker and Financial Broker.

The finance sector does not have the monopoly on wealth, so you should also look for the following: Solicitor, Barrister, Diplomat, QC, Broker, Trader, Oil Trader, Oil Broker, Shipbroker, Investor, Venture Capitalist, Racehorse Trainer, Actor, Footballer – indeed, anything you can think of that may yield a suitable result.

Your best option may be to export the relevant details (name and occupation) from your whole database into a spreadsheet and then sort the job titles in alphabetical order. Then you can go through them one by one, keeping the most promising ones and deleting the rest. This will also make sure you pick up (and correct!) any misspelled job titles – Fund Manger, Stckbroker, Barister – which inevitably creep into every database. Then import the finished list into your Prospect spreadsheet.

If you do not already capture parental occupation data when pupils register, then you should start doing so. And you should also send out an update form to alumni on a regular basis to enable them to add or update their career information. Further information about identifying occupations is given in the next chapter, section 4.3.

3.5 Email addresses

You can also identify someone's profession through their work email address.

As with the job title search, the best method to follow is to export the details of everyone on your database with an email address into a spreadsheet and then sort out the most promising emails (e.g. legal and accountancy firms, wealth management and other finance companies and also local businesses). To do this, I would sort them into alphabetical order by domain name and then go through the list one by one to identify those who may be wealthy. If you are unsure about a domain name, simply copy and paste it into your web browser to see what the company is.

To sort the list of email addresses by domain name, perform a 'find and replace' action (Ctrl F) on the list, putting ***@** in the **Find what** field and leaving the **Replace with** field blank. This will remove the prospect's name and the @ sign from the list of emails, leaving only the domain names which can then be sorted alphabetically.

It can take some time to sort through a list of email addresses, just as it can do to sort through job titles, but once you have deleted all the Yahoo, BT, Gmail and other generic email addresses, you should soon begin to see some potential prospects.

3.6 Property

The next technique to spot wealthy alumni is through the value of their property, based on the reasonable premise that someone in a £5m property is more likely to be capable of making a significant gift than someone in a £100,000 property.

An expensive property is no guarantee of wealth. If someone has lived in the same home for 50 or 60 years, the value of the property could have shot up since it was bought, even though the owner may actually have little disposable income. In cases such as these, you should consider cultivating them for a legacy.

Nor can you tell from a property website whether a person is mortgaged up to the eyeballs or not, but given that a mortgage is a product of their salary and the size of their deposit, the value of their property can give you some idea of their wealth.

How do you know if your alumnus is actually the owner of the house? One sure-fire way is to check the title deed of the property online using the Land Registry's website. This will also tell you whether they have a mortgage or not, so at the very least you can identify those who are mortgaged from those who are not. However, as this currently costs £3 per title deed, I would only carry out such a check if there is some doubt in your mind as to who owns the property. Another option is to search for the person's name and postcode using Google or Bing and see if they have made any planning applications. Many councils now list these online and they are a simple and free way to check who owns a property.

3.6.1 House names

One easy way to identify expensive property owners is to run a query which searches your database (or to be specific, just the first line of the address) for those names which are indicative of a large country house: Abbey, Castle, Court, Hall, House, Manor or Park. But be careful; this search will also bring up a large number of unwanted addresses (Manor Road, Castle Street, Park Hill), unless you specifically filter them out in your query.

If you find you cannot filter out these unwanted street names then import the whole list into a spreadsheet and sort the list A to Z. This will bring all the addresses with a number to the top of the list – 1 Manor Road, 2 Park Hill, 3 Castle Street – so that you can easily delete them, leaving only the house names you want.

Then you will need to check the value of the houses in your list to identify the expensive properties. I use Zoopla and Mouseprice to value property.

3.6.2 Postcodes

Another way to identify expensive properties on your database is to search for them by postcode.

This search is really only worthwhile if the majority of your pupils come from the local community. You can readily identify those parents and alumni who live in the most expensive streets in your area using websites like Mouseprice.co.uk, Zoopla.co.uk, Our Property and Prime Location, which list most expensive streets by postcode in towns throughout the UK.

My preferred website at the moment is Mouseprice. To find local postcodes with the most expensive properties, simply go to their website and select the 'Area Guide' tab at the top of the screen. Enter the postcode prefix for your particular area (e.g. RG4) and then select 'Most expensive' from the list of street rankings for that area. When the list of 30 postcodes appears, click on each street in turn to find the exact postcode. Then search for anyone in your database who lives at that postcode.

3.7 Tax havens

This technique identifies prospects who live in one of those countries with a very low level of tax which traditionally attract the wealthy. Simply search your database for anyone who lives in Guernsey, Jersey, Sark, Isle of Man, Liechtenstein, Luxembourg, Monaco, Switzerland, Bermuda or the Cayman islands.

As with private bank account holders, living in a tax haven is no guarantee that someone is wealthy, but those who live in one of these countries are more likely to have money than not.

3.8 Titled people

Searching for titled alumni or parents is another simple technique to identify wealthy prospects or those with good networks.

By titled, I mean both hereditary titles (Duke, Duchess, Marquess, Marchioness, Earl, Countess, Viscount, Viscountess) and life titles (Dame, Lady, Baroness, Lord and Sir).

Having a hereditary title is no guarantee of wealth. Although some hereditary peerages do come with an impressive amount of land and other assets, the phrase "asset-rich, cash-poor" exists for a reason; do not be fooled into thinking that a large mansion with a huge estate means the person must be a good prospect for a major gift. The same is true of those who are awarded life peerages, knighthoods or damehoods. But unlike those who gained their title through birth, this second group will have excelled in some way in their particular sphere of life, which has culminated in the award of a peerage, knighthood or damehood. They will have certain experiences, skills and connections which make them ideal as prospects – either for a major gift or for networking.

3.9 Wealth screening

Wealth screening companies compare your database with their own database of wealthy people (generally those with a net worth of £1m or more). They use a wide variety of publicly available sources (company and trust annual reports, rich lists, shareholder databases, national and regional newspapers, company websites and property data) to ensure that their data is as comprehensive and accurate as possible.

Subject to your individual circumstances, they will carry out an exploratory search for free, so that you know how many of your alumni are on their database. But if you want more detailed information you will have to pay. A <u>list of individual names</u> is the most basic information you can have, but if you wish to pay more you can find out about <u>wealth, gift capacity, philanthropic preferences</u> and motivations, their relationship to others on your database (and to your governors and senior personnel) and much more besides, assuming that the information is available for your alumni. The greater the information you would like, the more you will pay, and so you should think carefully about what level of information would be most useful to you given your budget.

A screening can be very useful, but do not think of it as something to be done *instead* of the other identification techniques described above. The two are complimentary. If you do have alumni who are worth £1m or more, a screening is likely to find them (as will some of the other techniques), but if you have alumni who fall below that level, but are still worth cultivating for a significant gift – I'm thinking here of doctors, accountants, solicitors and other professionals – then you will need to use the other techniques to identify them.

There are several different data screening companies, so it pays to shop around for the best deal. Ask them which schools they have worked with and then contact those schools directly to ask what they thought of the results. Did the search give them what they wanted? Was it competitively priced? How long did it take?

You may think, when reading through this chapter, "Oh, that search technique won't apply to my school."

You could not be more wrong.

Whilst there is no doubt that some of these searches will bring up more results for some schools than others, not all wealthy people went to Eton, Winchester or Harrow, or even to one of the other public schools. Given the growth and spread of wealth over the last 30 years, these searches are just as likely to bring up suitable alumni for a state school as they are for an independent one.

You never know what golden nugget may be buried in the ground until you take a look.

And I am well aware that several of these searches – those involving job title, email, house names and postcodes in particular – can be time consuming, but remember you are looking for people who can make a *major* gift to your school, so it is very much worth your while spending some time looking for them. Even half an hour a day will soon add up to a substantial amount of time over a period of several weeks. Just remember to always be methodical and keep everything in nice manageable chunks. This is why I recommend importing each list into a separate page of a spreadsheet; it helps to keep your work neat and tidy and it is very easy to show your progress to the Head or Appeal Chair, should they wish to be updated.

Websites

Information Commissioner's Office: https://ico.org.uk/

Land Registry: www.gov.uk/government/organisations/land-registry

Zoopla: www.zoopla.co.uk

Mouseprice: www.mouseprice.co.uk

Our Property: www.ourproperty.co.uk

Prime Location www.primelocation.com

Prospecting for Benefactors

4

Identifying prospects through other sources

4.1 Paying school fees in advance ✗

Asking your bursar or finance director for a list of those who have paid one or more years' school fees in advance is a quick and easy way to create a list of prospects. Aside from the convenience of paying fees in one lump sum, there is a good financial reason for doing so, which will be attractive to those who can afford it (i.e. the Fees in Advance Scheme that some schools run).

If you are unfamiliar with the scheme, it works like this. The parents make a lump sum equivalent to one or more years' fees to the school. The school then invests the lump sum in low-risk investments, the returns on which are tax free for the school because of its charitable status. If the parents had made the same investment, they would have got a much smaller return because of the higher rate tax they undoubtedly pay. The parents and the school then split the benefit. In return for paying upfront the parents are given what the school classes as a discount. And the school keeps whatever is remaining of the returns once they have offered the discount to the parents.

Whilst paying for fees in advance is no guarantee of wealth (the payment may have been made after receiving a lump sum as redundancy, for example) it is much more likely than not that those parents who pay several years' fees in advance are wealthy.

4.2 Biographies

Who's Who contains autobiographies of some 33,000 "noteworthy and influential" people in the UK and abroad. Debrett's *People of Today* contains autobiographies of 25,000 of "the UK's most influential and successful people." Together, they can provide you with a quick and easy way to create a list of prospects. Simply search for your school in the online versions and see who comes up! Both books are available without subscription through library membership.

To find your local library go to **www.gov.uk** and search for library services. This will bring up the link to Local Library Services, from which you can identify your local library and the research resources they provide. If you are after a particular resource, your local library should be able to advise you as to the nearest library which offers that resource.

Although being listed in *Who's Who* and *People of Today* is not a sign of wealth, it is a sign that your prospect has been successful in some sphere of life and this success may have brought financial gain with it. You will have to use your own judgement, based upon their career, seniority, directorships and any other information your find to determine whether they are a prospect or not.

Do bear in mind that if your school has recently merged or changed its name, those who attended before this happened will most likely (and understandably) use the name of the school when they were there. And some people use abbreviations; Sch rather than School being the most common. *Who's Who* has an advanced search facility which allows you to search in just the Education field, which you may find useful.

You need to search both books as they do differ in their content. *People of Today* is "dedicated to contemporary achievement" and so entrants are not guaranteed a place for life, unlike entrants in *Who's Who*, who are not just there for life, but beyond! Once deceased, they pass to *Who Was Who*, which has some 90,000 entries dating back to 1897. Many people are listed in *Who's Who* and *People of Today*, but there are some who are only listed in one. What is the same is that each entrant writes their own autobiography, which means you can be sure of the veracity of the information.

4.3 LinkedIn and Facebook

LinkedIn is the leading business-oriented social networking website with over 300 million members, each of whom has a profile and many of whom list the school they attended. If you do not already have a school presence on LinkedIn (and the more fun-oriented social networking site Facebook), then you must create them. And if someone else has created one for your school (as old pupils sometimes do) then you really should take ownership of it (in the nicest possible way).

Both resources can be a useful source of prospects, but it is LinkedIn which is really the specialist resource for this sort of thing, as many people put detailed career information on their profiles; the sort of information which they do not put on Facebook. And if you already have a group set up for your school, then you can search for alumni by profession, and then target those with an interesting profession/career (see section 3.4 for a reminder of wealth-related job titles and professions).

To find people on LinkedIn who went to your school then write out the following URL into your browser,

www.linkedin.com/edu/alumni?name=School+name+here

replacing the words School+name+here with your school's name.

For my old school, Abingdon School, I would use the following:

www.linkedin.com/edu/alumni?name=Abingdon+School

And for the John Madejski Academy (in my home town of Reading) I would use:

www.linkedin.com/edu/alumni?name=John+Madejski+Academy

What this does is instruct LinkedIn to list all the people who use these words in the education section of their profile and, more importantly, to list them in such a way that you can sort them by **Where they live**, **Where they work** and **What they do** (the actual column headings that LinkedIn uses). You can also restrict your search to those who left school more than 10 or 15 years ago, excluding those who will not yet have progressed very far in their careers.

What you then need to do is to sort out the list of people (which may run to several thousand) by clicking on either **Where they work** (to pick out those companies most likely to pay well, such as merchant banks, accountancy firms and solicitors) or **What they do** (to pick out those careers most likely to pay well, such as finance, law and accountancy). Do keep a record (on the spreadsheet, for example) of which companies and professions you have looked at, to avoid forgetting what you have done and duplicating your work – or accidentally missing out a company or profession.

The final stage involves checking each person's profile and deciding, then and there, whether you want to add them to your spreadsheet of prospects or not. You will find that people will fall into one of three categories. Those who are clearly prospects (CEOs and others obviously in senior positions), those who are clearly not prospects (the majority of the people you find, I suspect) and those who may fall into either category, but a quick look on their LinkedIn profile does not give you enough information to know. If you already have a large list of prospects from the techniques listed in the previous chapters, then I would ignore those who you are unsure

Prospecting for Benefactors

about. If you only have a very few prospects so far, then I would add the 'unsure' people to the prospect spreadsheet and look at them in more detail when you come to qualify your prospects.

Using LinkedIn in this way is a very simple and effective way of identifying prospects, but it does have one shortcoming; it may bring up a lot of 'false positives'. These can occur in two ways. When I search for Abingdon School, it lists all the people who use the words 'Abingdon' and 'School' in their education section, which means that as well as Abingdon School, the following schools are also selected:

- John Mason School, Abingdon
- Larkmead School, Abingdon
- St Helen & St Katherine School, Abingdon
- Our Lady's School, Abingdon
- Fitzharry's School, Abingdon
- Abingdon High School

Practically speaking, this is not a serious problem, as you will need to look at each alumnus individually anyway, once you come to qualify your prospects, so you will be able to pick out those who went to a different school before you get to the stage of considering them a serious prospect. And it may not be a problem at all for you, if your school has a unique name.

The second way in which false positives may occur is if your school has the same name as one in the USA (or anywhere else in the world). Abingdon High School, Virginia, was unknown to me until I began writing this book! To remove these unwanted schools from your search, simply click on United Kingdom in the **Where they live** column. This is not a perfect solution – anyone from your school not currently living in the UK will be removed as well, and anyone who went to the foreign school but who now lives in the UK will be included – but it is a quick and simple way to remove the great majority of the false positives.

4.4 Newspapers

As a general rule, newspapers do not run stories about people unless there is something 'newsworthy' about them and one of those things is money. For this reason, finding national or local newspaper articles mentioning your alumni can be a very useful way of uncovering prospects.

You can search many newspapers online simply by using Google or Bing. But these search engines do not capture everything and so for local newspapers it is worth your while searching the newspaper's own website. You should also use the news archive NewsBank, available without subscription through library membership. NewsBank is a collection of 60 or so national and local newspaper archives dating back between 15 and 30 years, depending upon the newspaper, and is a very useful resource for prospect research.

To maximise your chances of finding relevant articles, imagine how an alumnus of your school might be mentioned in a news article and phrase your search string accordingly.

"Former [school name] pupil"
"Former [school name] student"
"Former pupil of [School name]"
"Former student of [School name]"
"[school name] old boy/girl"
"[school name]" "a former pupil of the school"
"[school name]" "a former student of the school"
"went to [school name]"
"attended [school name]"

If your school is one of those which has changed its name, or amalgamated with another school, do not forget to search for people using both names.

4.5 Local businessmen and women

I have seen both state and private schools receive support from people who lived locally – even if they did not attend that school – because they recognised that the school serves the local community of which they are a part.

The extent to which you can make use of local goodwill will depend upon your own individual circumstances. I imagine that a single state school in a small town will have much greater success attracting local support than an independent school in a large town with several state schools. But never say never.

As with the search for alumni in section 3.3, you can find news articles about local businessmen and women, entrepreneurs and other successful locals by searching Google or Bing, or your local newspaper's own website. As with the previous search, to maximise your chances of success, imagine how the news article might be phrased and phrase your search string accordingly or check out the latest copy of your local paper for any articles about local businessmen and women and see what phrases they use to describe them.

As an example, to find local businessmen and women in my home town of Reading, I would try the following:

"local tycoon" "Reading"
"local businessman" "Reading"
"local businesswoman" "Reading"
"Born in Reading"
"born in Reading" "businessman"
"Reading-born tycoon/businessman/woman"
"Reading-born philanthropist"
"Local philanthropist" "Reading"

Another way to find local businessmen and women is to search *Who's Who*. Simply put your town into the search field and the website brings up a list of results and asks if you would like to filter them by Names, family, Education, Career, Recreations, Address or All. If you click on Address then the website lists people who live in your town. You then need to go through the list one by one, looking for suitable businessmen and women.

Websites

Who's Who: www.ukwhoswho.co.uk

People of Today:
www.debretts.com/people-today-index

Know UK: www.knowuk.co.uk

Local Library Services: www.gov.uk/local-library-services

LinkedIn: www.linkedin.com

Facebook: www.facebook.com

5

Qualifying Prospects

5.1 Qualification as triage

Qualification is the stage at which you decide how good each prospect is, rejecting those who are unsuitable and ranking those who remain, so that you know who to approach first and for what level of donation.

The process of qualification is not about in-depth research. Rather, it is about being able, as quickly and easily as you can, to decide whether a prospect may be capable of making a major gift and at what level (and if they are not, do they know someone who is?) A useful analogy is that of triage in hospitals. In the process of triage, the hospital is not concerned with treating/curing the patient there and then, but with ascertaining the extent of the person's injuries and the best course of action to take. It is about making quick, accurate, effective decisions. Qualification should be the same. You do not want to spend hours delving into your prospect's career; you just want to be able to make as quick a decision as you can then move on to the next person.

Some of your prospects will require very little further qualification (e.g. private bank account holders, previous major donors and <u>senior company directors</u> who are <u>known</u> to one of your <u>governors</u> or someone from your <u>alumni committee</u> or <u>parents association</u>). Most others will require more research, especially those who are unknown to your governors, alumni committee or parents association.

To research your prospects effectively you will need to become familiar with using a variety of web-based research resources. What I suggest you do, as I take you through the resources you will need, is create a folder in your web browser called **Research Resources** and bookmark all the resources you will need in this folder, so you have them readily to hand. And **I do urge you to join a library**. Library membership can provide you with free access to a wide variety of online resources.

The order in which you use the various research resources to qualify a prospect really depends upon how much information you have about the prospect in the first place. But there is merit in following the same general plan for each prospect, at least until you are confident in what you are doing. For this reason, I have created a Qualification Flow Chart (see Appendix C) which takes you through the basic steps of qualifying a prospect, with reminders as to the sort of information you are looking for at each step. It is not designed to be followed rigidly, but rather to act as a guide and aide memoir, to be adapted as necessary depending on where your research takes you. Nor do you necessarily need to go through each step of the chart. In fact, it has been designed so that you should not need to in order to qualify most of your prospects, as the easiest and most obvious wealth indicators are found in the earlier steps. Once you are satisfied a prospect has money, stop and move on to your next prospect, do not go all the way through the chart. Save that for any further research you wish to do whilst you are cultivating them and definitely before you actually ask them for money.

You may find it helpful to add the steps in the flow chart to your prospect spreadsheet as column titles (Property value, Companies House, Who's Who and so on). Then you can fill out the spreadsheet for each prospect as you go through the steps in the flow chart. This will also act as an excellent record of which resources you have looked at to qualify the prospect and which you still need to look at if you want to research them in more detail.

5.2 Check your database

The first step is to look each prospect up on your database (if you do not have one, then pass on to the next step). The more you can learn about your prospect before you look to the internet, the better; you may learn valuable information about their career or attitude towards the school. You may even learn something about them which causes you to remove them from your list (most obviously, if there is a note on their record saying they do not wish to be asked for money).

Specifically, look out for the following:

- Do you know their profession/job title/seniority?
- Have they ever made any donations to the school (and was it on a cheque from a private bank)?
- How old are they? (Generally speaking, the older the donor, the more likely they are to give).
- How many children do they have?
- Are their children still living with them or are they independent? (People tend to give more if they are no longer paying for their children – or their grandchildren!)
- Did the children attend your school as well?
- Have they attended any events?
- Have they had any communication with the school and if so, how much information did they provide? (The more information they provided, the more likely they are to be warm to the school).
- Have they said if they have kept in touch with their classmates?
- What year did they leave?

The answers to all these questions can give you a good idea of how they feel about the school and so how likely they will be to want to support the school and who may be the best person to approach them.

5.3 Property value

The next step is to look up the value of the prospect's home. On its own, knowing this can only tell you so much, unless the property is very expensive (over £5m) or very cheap (under £100k). A very expensive property, even if you allow for a mortgage, is a good sign of wealth, just as a very inexpensive property is (probably) a sign that there is not much wealth, but for properties in between, you will need to view it alongside the other wealth indicators you have been able to find and make your own judgement.

Property websites such as Zoopla and Mouseprice keep records of property sales going back several years, allowing you to learn what someone's house may be worth and possibly what they paid for it. And as I mentioned in chapter 3, it is possible to find out if the property is mortgaged or owned outright by ordering a copy of the Title Deed from the Land Registry.

If you are unsure as to whether your prospect still lives at the address you have for him or you only have a partial address, you can check the electoral roll. I use 192.com which has over 200 million records taken from current and past electoral rolls. 192.com provides some information for free, but more comprehensive information & searches require credits, but they are not expensive. 192.com also contains information from Companies House and matches it with information from the electoral roll and home telephone directory. If you are after a totally free service, BT's Phone Book provides name and address information along with the person's phone number (assuming they are not ex-directory).

5.4 Companies House

Companies House is responsible for registering and dissolving limited companies, registering the information companies are legally required to supply, and making that information available to the public. It is therefore an essential resource for company and director information. Depending upon the type of company, you may be able to discover a great deal about a prospect's wealth, based on their current and past directorships (which will give you a good idea of their career and seniority), information about their shareholdings and whether the companies of which they are a director or shareholder are profitable or not.

The best way to access Companies House data used to be through Companies House Direct, for which one had to pay a subscription. But in early-2015, Companies House launched a 'beta' version of their new free service. At the time of writing (July 2015), this beta site does not offer all the functionality of Companies House Direct, but the plan is that this free service will completely replicate and replace the subscription service currently offered by Companies House Direct.

There are also a variety of other online company and director databases that all source their information from Companies House and have the advantage of providing information in a more convenient format. Much of the information they provide is free, but for more detailed information you will have to pay. The two I recommend you use are Company Check and DueDil. Each has its strengths and weaknesses. Duedil provides the most detailed financial information, and for those companies that are required to register such details, it will allow you to know a company's turnover, profit (or loss), total and net assets, shareholder funds and directors remuneration (which will enable you to work out what the average director's pay is, by dividing the remuneration by the number of directors). What DueDil does not give you (unless you pay to upgrade) is the names of shareholders, parental or subsidiary companies or directors' addresses. Company Check, on the other hand, only shows a summary of a company's finances, but *does* list shareholders, parental and subsidiary companies and directors' addresses. Consequently, I suggest you familiarise yourself with both websites and use them as necessary. But do not forget Companies House Direct and the new free beta website. Unlike the other sites, Companies House Direct lists past addresses and so if you can only find a company address for your prospect on Company Check, then look for a home address on Companies House Direct and then check to see if this address is still current through the electoral roll (192.com).

Whichever company resource you use, the amount of information available to you will vary depending upon the size and type of company. For many companies, you will only find very limited financial information and for others, no financial information at all. In such cases you will need to make a judgement based upon the company website and what information you can find from an internet search. Even after all this, you may be none the wiser as to how much money the company makes.

But for other companies, especially larger companies, extensive financial information will be available, giving you an estimate of (some of) the prospect's wealth if he or she is a director or shareholder in the company. If the prospect is a director and/or shareholder of a public limited company (one that makes its shares available to the public), then it should be possible to get a very accurate idea of the prospect's salary (it will be listed in the annual report) and/or the value of the prospect's shareholding in the company (get the latest share price by Googling the company's name and share price and multiply this by the number of shares the prospect owns). The share trading website Digital Look also provides detailed company information regarding directors, their shareholdings and recent deals.

For private limited companies, the share price will not be listed. But you can look at the company's latest financial figures from Companies House and, specifically, the figure for Shareholder Funds or Net Worth. As a (very) general rule of thumb, you can use this figure to value the company, but to be really meaningful this must be qualified by the profits (or losses) the company has made in the last few years (one year can be misleading), whether turnover is expanding or contracting and how the sector in which the company sits is doing generally. I.e. would someone be willing to buy it for the net asset value or would they expect to pay more – or less?

So, if a company has shareholder funds of £10m and your prospect owns a 50% share, they own, theoretically, £5m worth of shares. But if the company has been making losses of hundreds of thousands of pounds for several years, and in a declining industry, will anyone want to pay them anywhere close to that £5m for their shares? Very unlikely. On the other hand, if the company has been making *profits* of several hundred thousand pounds over the last few years, and in an expanding market, the prospect will want, and be right to expect, much more than £5m for their 50% share of the company.

Trying to value a company in this way is complicated by the fact that some companies have very low net assets and yet (if they are trading in the skills and expertise of their workforce, rather than tangible assets) may make substantial profits and be worth a great deal of money to the right buyer.

If you cannot find a company on Companies House, it may be that your prospect owns or works for a company that does not need to be listed (e.g. a sole trader). Another option is that the company trades under a different name to that by which it is generally known. Try looking on the company's website to see if they use a different trading name. If it is not immediately apparent from the company's home page (as it is with some companies) then look for a page marked as 'Privacy Policy' or 'Terms and Conditions', as such pages usually list the company's registered name.

When searching for a prospect on Companies House, DueDil or Company Check it is best to use the prospect's full name, otherwise you may find yourself having to search through hundreds of directors with the same name and not know which (if any) is yours. Having a full name means you can separate John Mortimer Doe from the other people called John Doe. If you only know he is John Doe, you can identify him using his date of birth, as all of these websites either list the date of birth next to a director's name in the results table or allow you to filter the names by date of birth. And if you have a full name *and* a date of birth, you can be certain you have the right person.

If you are having trouble finding someone on one of these websites, then use Google or Bing to search for them using one of the following phrases:

"John Mortimer Doe"
John Doe 1966
John Doe NW3

If the prospect is listed in Companies House, this should bring up the relevant page on Company Check or one of the other Companies House websites. If it does not bring up any results for one of these websites, then it is unlikely your prospect is listed as a director in Companies House.

5.5 Who's Who & People of Today

It is quick and easy to check *Who's Who* and *People of Today*. Remember that both resources are available without subscription through library membership. Or, if you have carried out the search in section 4.2, you can simply check each of your alumni prospects against this list. You will still need to check for parents manually, though, as they will not have been found with that search.

Remember that being listed is not itself a sign of wealth, but it is a sign that your prospect has been successful in some sphere of life and this success may have brought financial gain with it. Their career, seniority, directorships and any other wealth indicators will help you to decide whether they are a prospect or not. You should also note what their family situation is. Is the prospect single, married or divorced? Do they have children and if so, are they still dependent upon their parents? A prospect who is single with no children will have more disposable wealth than one who is married with children at school or university.

ThePeerage.com is another biographical resource, providing a genealogical survey of the peerage of Britain as well as the royal families of Europe. It can be very useful for researching titled families.

Another excellent resource is Know UK, which provides access to more than 100 biographies, directories, encyclopaedias and other reference works, including *People of Today* and other useful resources. And it is available free through library membership.

5.6 LinkedIn

LinkedIn, the business-oriented social networking website, is an invaluable resource. It has over 300 million members, each of whom has a profile, and many of whom list their full career history, as well as the university and/or school they attended.

Use the following phrase to find prospects on LinkedIn:

"Jane Doe" LinkedIn

The quotes are important as you want Google/Bing to search for the exact phrase Jane Doe and ignore LinkedIn pages it finds with the words Jane and Doe, which may refer to, for example, the LinkedIn record of Mary Doe, who works for Jane Smith Ltd.

A LinkedIn profile can be a great source of information about your prospect, telling you not only who they currently work for, but very often who they worked for before and for how long. It can give you a good idea of their career progression (including non-directorship positions which will not appear on Companies House) and allow you to estimate the level of wealth they may have. Some people also list outside interests, including charitable interests, which can give you an idea of how philanthropic they are.

Once you know the prospect's company, you can search for their name with the company name on Google or Bing to see if it brings up a company biography.

5.7 Trustees of charitable trusts

The Charity Commission's Register of Charities contains details of registered charities in England and Wales. Very useful for finding out who is a trustee of their own charitable trust (a sign of wealth) or a trustee of someone else's trust (still good to know). The Office of the Scottish Charity Regulator is responsible for keeping an accurate register of Scottish Charities. The website has a very useful advanced search facility but the level of detail provided is inferior to that provided by the Charity Commission.

To determine if your prospect is a trustee, use one of the searches below (trustees are often listed on the Register of Charities under their full name, and so searching for this should bring up your prospect and not any other John Does who may be trustees of other charities. On the other hand, if he is listed merely as John Doe, then you will need to try the second search):

"John Mortimer Doe" opencharities.org
"John Doe" opencharities.org

These searches actually bring up results from the website Open Charities, which is just like the Register of Charities (from which it sources its information) with one distinct advantage. You can search its contents through a search engine, allowing you to find who may be a trustee of a charitable trust more easily than using the search facility of the Register of Charities, which only allows you to search by charity name. Moreover, the helpful people who run the site provide a link from the charity's page on their website to the charity's pages on the Charity Commission website.

A prospect with their own charitable trust is a definite indicator of wealth. Trusts over a certain size have to send annual accounts to the Charity Commission and these can tell you a great deal about the prospect's wealth and philanthropic interests. Many charitable trusts list the previous years' donations individually, which is ideal, but even if they do not, for all but the smallest trusts, you will be able to see their annual expenditure, which can give you some indication of the prospect's wealth.

If the prospect does not have their own charitable trust but is a trustee of another charitable trust then this is still very useful to know. Even if the trust states in its accounts that it does not support education, or schools specifically, do not be put off. Many charitable trusts leave aside a small proportion of their annual expenditure to spend on a few of the trustees' favourite causes, some of which may fall outside their official remit, and so you may be able to persuade your prospect to include your school amongst these.

5.8 Other philanthropy

Hard evidence of philanthropy is difficult to find for most prospects, but many charities list major donors in their annual reports, and JustGiving and other fundraising websites list donors' names, so it is always worth looking for them. Most major gifts to charity are made by the wealthy, but not all of them. People of limited means do sometimes make one-off major gifts to a particular cause or charity close to their heart (such as their old school). But for the most part, a large donation is a good indicator of wealth.

To identify any philanthropic activity by your prospect, use the following searches:

"Jane Doe" "trustee"
"Jane Doe" "charitable"
"Jane Doe" "donation"
"Jane Doe" "Thank you" "donors"

It is quite rare to know exactly what someone has given to a particular charity, but you can often get a very good idea if a prospect is listed as a donor in a charity's annual report. Some charities do actually list major donors by gift band (£5k-£9.9, £10k-£24.9, £25k-£49k, etc.) which is very helpful in telling you (approximately) what each donor has given. More usually, they are listed by category (Bronze, Silver, Gold, Platinum is one common grouping, as is Friends, Partners, Benefactors, Patrons). Or they will be listed alphabetically, with no indication of what each person's gift is. But the fact that your prospect appears in such a list tells you they have made a substantial donation. How substantial? Probably at least £5,000 or £10,000 is the cut-off point for many charities, but it will be higher for some. You can sometimes learn what this cut-off point is from the charity's website, if they have a dedicated 'major donor' page which explains the benefits you can receive as a major donor. To attract the right level of donor, the charity may specify what level of gift they consider to be a major gift. Once you know this, you will know *at least* what level of gift the donors in their 'Thank you' list made.

5.9 News archives

The importance of unencumbered investigative journalism is recognised by the Data Protection Act such that journalists do not have to adhere to the act in the way that you and I do. This means that their articles and interviews often go into a greater level of detail than any other research resource. If you cannot find out anything about a prospect, or you want to confirm something you have read elsewhere from an unreliable source, then you should carry out a search on a news archive.

As well as confirming what you already know, you may learn valuable information about a prospect not found elsewhere; about their career, their personal life, what they thought of the school, their interests and hobbies and how they help the local community – or not!

As I stated in section 4.4, I use the online newspaper archive, NewsBank, available without subscription through library membership. Many local and nearly all national newspapers also have their own online archives. Do also check your local newspaper's website as it may not be covered by NewsBank.

5.10 Practise makes perfect

And now it is your turn. Beginning with your first list of prospects, you must go down the list, looking at each prospect in turn, using the flow diagram and the appropriate research resources to help you identify the salary, shareholdings or other wealth indicators necessary to qualify your prospect.

There is a great temptation, when you want to find something out about someone, to just put their name into Google and see what comes up. If you are really daring, you may also try Bing or Yahoo.

Please do try to resist this urge when qualifying your prospects. This is not proper research and can easily lead you astray.

I know it is quick and easy, but that is the danger. In your haste to qualify your prospects as quickly and easily as you can, you are in danger of treating the first results you find as the most relevant or accurate. But this ignores a fundamental fact about search engine results: they are ranked in the order that the search engine is programmed to order them, not in the order that will bring up the most relevant or accurate results for you.

To be a little more specific, results from Google will vary depending on where your computer is based and your previous search history. A search on Google (and Bing) may also bring up all sorts of prompts, in the form of predictive text, which may confuse and confound your search before you have even begun. The search engine is trying to predict what you are searching for, which can sometimes be useful (if it brings up your prospect's name with a company name) but can just as easily throw you off (if it brings up a different person with the same name as your prospect and the company *they* work for). To appreciate how much this can throw you off, just imagine one of your alumni is called Richard Branson. A search of his name will return a great many results, but (nearly) all of them will be for the wrong person!

By beginning your research with the reliable resources I list, you will greatly minimise your chances of being led astray by a general web search. Remember the old idiom 'a lie can travel half way around the world while the truth is putting on its shoes'. The internet is awash with lies and half-truths, reported on multiple different websites, so do not think that just because something appears many times it is accurate. Websites are like people: some are reliable, some less so, and some are to be avoided altogether. If you base your research around the resources I list, you should go a long way towards avoiding the unreliable ones or spotting them for what they are.

You may have noticed that I did not include Wikipedia in my list of resources. The reason for this is that whilst Wikipedia can sometimes be wonderful for biographical information, it can also be very unsatisfactory. It is written and edited by a wide variety of people, with different skill-sets, knowledge and experience, so you cannot rely equally on everything it contains. Wikipedia articles are supposed to be sourced, so follow the sources if they are there, and make your own judgement as to how reliable they are. If there are no sources, try to confirm the information from a reliable source – or treat it with great caution.

You should also be wary of websites that use automated methods to trawl the internet for biographical information and present it as if it was collated by a person. Such sites may contain valuable information but they can also be out of date with unreliable or unverifiable information. Again, try to confirm the information from a reliable source. Salary sites should also be treated with caution as many of them rely on self-reporting and so are completely unverifiable. Use them as a rough guide by all means, but check them against newspaper and trade journal articles about salaries or job adverts related to the job in question.

Even more unreliable are weblogs and other personal websites that do not source the information or opinions they contain. As before, look to confirm any interesting information from a reliable source.

Company websites on the other hand are generally sound, but do bear in mind that for many companies, their website will show you what the company wants you to see. A company may be close to insolvency, but have a lovely, colourful, thriving website! Companies House will give a truer picture of the company's fortunes than any website.

In conclusion, when you come to qualify your prospects, it is the more reliable resources with which you should start - Companies House, the Register of Charities, the electoral roll, BT.com, *Who's Who, People of Today*, company annual reports and company websites - leaving the less reliable for any gaps or supplementary information.

Am I saying that I never simply chuck someone's name into Google to see what comes up? Of course I do, but I've been doing this for years and know what to look out for. I won't be taken in by a website containing detailed, but unsourced, information about my prospect. At least, I hope I won't! Everyone gets caught out now and then; the trick is to use reliable sources as much as you can to minimise the risk and always try to confirm information from questionable sources using a reliable source.

It can become monotonous, checking prospect after prospect, and time-consuming when you have other responsibilities, so I would aim to qualify your prospects in one or two hour chunks, so that you can really zip through them before fatigue or boredom sets in – that is when mistakes will be made.

Do, do, do keep a written record of who you have looked at and what you have found (this is what the prospect spreadsheet is for, after all). If you wish, you can add the information you find to your database (especially full name and date of birth and to correct outdated, incomplete or incorrect information) but remember we are at the stage of qualification; anything more may slow you down. As you go down the list, mark those who are obviously wealthy, and also those who are clearly not (or for whom you can find no information) and leave the rest to come back to at a later date. At this early stage, we are aiming to identify the best prospects; the 'maybes' can wait until later in your fundraising campaign, when you are more confident and experienced in what you are doing and so more capable of making a sound judgement about who is probably wealthy and who is not.

5.11 Troubleshooting

There may be occasions when you can find out little or nothing about your prospect, despite all the resources at your disposal. And it may be that there is simply nothing to find; that is the case with some people, even people with money. But there are some other possibilities that you should consider...

- Check how the prospect's name is spelt. It is easy to misspell an unusual or unfamiliar name. Are you using their first name, when they use their second name, or using their full name when they go by a nickname?
- If a woman, do they go by their married name, their maiden name or a combination of the two? Professional women often continue to use their maiden name in business circles. Separated or divorced women may also revert to their maiden name.
- Is there an email address that you can check? Some people use a completely different name to their given name and their email address may reflect this (this is more common with actors and singers).
- Finally, pay attention when searching for foreign names. In some countries and cultures, the surname comes before the first name or the father's surname may differ from the mothers.

If you do not have an address for an alumnus there are several steps you can take to find either a work or a home address.

If you know the prospect's full name or date of birth, check Companies House Direct. This will provide at least one address, even if for some people it is a service (i.e. work) address. If there is a link to 'other addresses' then select it as it may bring up a home address which is still valid for the person (but which they do not wish to have listed as their primary address).

Check the address (or addresses) you find on Companies House with those on the electoral roll or BT's phone directory to determine if the person still lives there.

If you cannot find the person you want, then try looking for their spouse and/or children. Celebrities and others in the public eye, such as prominent businessmen and women, are increasingly requesting that councils do not pass on their personal data, including their name and address, when they sign the electoral roll. But sometimes their spouse or children do not think to make such a request, enabling you to identify their home address.

If you think you know the area where the alumni has moved to, you can try searching Google or Bing with their name and the area. This may find planning permission documents, which councils are increasingly posting online, which could confirm the prospect's address.

Finally, check *Who's Who* and *People of Today*. If they have an entry it will almost certainly have a contact address and it may be a home address.

Websites

192.com: www.192.com

BT's Phone Book: www.bt.com

Companies House Direct: http://direct.companieshouse.gov.uk

Companies House 'beta' version: https://beta.companieshouse.gov.uk

Company Check: http://companycheck.co.uk

DueDil: www.duedil.com

Digital Look: www.digitallook.com

Who's Who: www.ukwhoswho.co.uk

People of Today: www.debretts.com/people-today-index

Know UK: www.knowuk.co.uk

ThePeerage.com: www.thepeerage.com

Register of Charities: www.gov.uk/government/organisations/charity-commission

Office of the Scottish Charity Regulator: www.oscr.org.uk

Open Charities: http://opencharities.org

Newsbank: various websites depending upon library membership

Prospecting for Benefactors

6

Ranking Prospects

6.1 The gift pyramid

Why do you need to rank your prospects?

There are two main reasons. The first is that the tried and tested method of raising money for a capital appeal is to create what is called a gift pyramid. A gift pyramid is simply a list of gifts with your lead gift (your biggest gift) at the top and smaller gifts underneath. If you imagine the number of gifts at each stage corresponding to the number of bricks in a building, then you can appreciate that the gifts will form an approximate pyramid shape.

Gift level	Gifts needed	Prospects needed	Total per level
£100,000	1	4	£100,000
£75,000	2	8	£150,000
£50,000	5	20	£250,000
£25,000	10	30	£250,000
£10,000	20	60	£200,000
Smaller	Many	Many	£50,000
			£1,000,000

In order to fill your gift pyramid, you must rank your prospects by their capacity to make a gift, to ensure you have the right number of prospects at the right level.

I have made several assumptions with my gift pyramid. The first is that the lead gift will be 10% of the total target. 10% of your total is a good lead gift to aim for, whatever the size of your appeal. The second assumption is that for every 3 to 4 prospects you find, you will only get a donation from one of them. 3 to 4 prospects for 1 donor is the rule of thumb that I use, but the actual number of prospects that you need may be higher or lower depending upon the quality of the prospects you find. The third assumption is that you will find many more prospects willing to make a lower donation than a higher one, based upon the obvious fact that the more money you ask for, the fewer the people who will be able to (or want to) afford it.

The second reason for ranking your prospects is to ensure that you begin your appeal by approaching those most likely to support it with a lead gift; those at the highest gift level who are warmest to the school and with most affinity for the appeal. Fundraising appeals are hard enough without making the job even more difficult by chasing unenthusiastic prospects. Once you have some lead gifts, others will be motivated to give, including those who may have initially been wary of supporting your appeal. This is especially true if they know any of your lead donors, although this information may remain confidential in the earlier stages of the appeal.

The ranking process therefore involves taking your prospects through 3 stages.

1. Ranking prospects by gift capacity
2. Ranking prospects by warmth to the school
3. Ranking prospects by affinity to the fundraising appeal

6.2 Gift capacity

It is vital to rank your prospects by gift capacity, so that you know whether you have enough prospects to populate your gift pyramid. If you group your prospects into gift levels, using the gift pyramid as a guide as to what levels you need, then you can keep an easy tally of how many prospects you have and how many you need. So, for the £1,000,000 gift pyramid, I would use the following 6 levels:

1. £100,000 +
2. £75,001 - £100,000
3. £50,001 - £75,000
4. £25,001 - £50,000
5. £10,001 - £25,000
6. £1,000 - £10,000

If I had a prospect with a gift capacity of £30,000, then I would put them into level 3. A prospect with a gift capacity of £5,000 would go into level 5 and a prospect with a gift capacity of £500,000 would go straight into level 1.

How should you rank your prospects? For those for whom you have accurate financial or philanthropic information, it is simply a matter of putting them in the appropriate level depending upon their wealth, salary or donation history. In common with many other fundraisers, I use the following general guidelines to help me arrive at a base figure:

1. If you have a good estimate of your prospect's wealth, knock off two zeroes and use that as your gift capacity. Or, as it is usually more formally stated, assume gift capacity to be 1% of the prospect's total assets.
2. If you know your prospect's salary, then assume gift capacity to be 5% of that figure.
3. If you know what your prospect has given in the past, then use that figure (or range) to come to a gift capacity figure, subject to what else you have learnt about the prospect's finances.

These guidelines are designed only as a starting point. I will increase or decrease the gift capacity figure they provide depending upon the individual prospect's circumstances (children at school or university, retired or still working, plus any intelligence I can pick up from friends or acquaintances of the prospect).

This may seem a bit hit and miss, but asking for a donation is all about negotiation. It's very rare that you will know exactly what a prospect will a) be able to give and b) actually want to give to you. What you do want, though, is a starting figure and this is what these guidelines provide.

For those for whom you do not have accurate financial or philanthropic information, you will have to use your intelligence, and a bit of common sense, to make an educated guess based upon the type and number of wealth indicators your prospect satisfies.

6.3 Warmth and affinity

Gift capacity on its own only tells you so much. A prospect may have the capacity to make a gift of £100,000 to your school, but have absolutely no inclination to do so. It is therefore vital to know how warm your prospects are before you approach them for a gift.

Unlike wealth, warmth is quite easy to work out. The greater the contact the prospect has had with the school (attending events, replying to invitations, keeping in contact with other alumni), the warmer they will be. The greater the donations they have given (both in size and frequency), the warmer they will be. You should not expect an alumnus who has had little or no contact with the school to be as warm as one who has had regular contact, and an alumnus who has had regular contact and given one or more donations will be warmer still. But do not worry if your chosen alumnus appears to have little or no warmth towards the school; they may still look back on the school fondly, but have had no reason to stay in contact. Once you start to engage them in the school's activities, their warmth – or lack of it - should become apparent. Alumni who do not wish to have anything to do with the school will be quick to say so.

It is easy to overcomplicate things, so I would have a simple 1, 2, 3 number system to rank your prospects by warmth.

1. Cold
2. Warm
3. Hot

Those with little or no contact with the school start at 1. Those who have attended the odd event, been in recent communication or even made a donation are at 2. And those who have attended several events, made several donations or been in frequent and recent contact are at 3. Adjust as necessary to fit in with your own school.

Warmth is one thing, but why would someone who studied physics, chemistry and biology at A level want to support your new theatre appeal, no matter how warm they are to the school? You must not ignore how much *affinity* your prospect will have for the particular appeal you are planning. If you are raising money for a new Theatre, a lukewarm prospect who excelled at the arts will probably have a greater affinity for the appeal than a warm prospect who studied the sciences and became a doctor. Many fundraising campaigns will appeal to all warm donors, of course, but even so it is a good idea to be aware of where a prospect's particular affinity may lie. Did he/she study science or arts? Were they sporty and if so, which sports? What hobbies or clubs did they belong to?

As with warmth, I would have a simple 3 tier system to rank your prospects by affinity.

1. Unknown or no affinity
2. Some affinity
3. Strong affinity.

You can record warmth and affinity on your Prospect spreadsheet – although it may be getting rather crowded by now – or in a separate spreadsheet (see Appendix D), which will make it easier to show others. Do remember to update warmth and affinity scores as necessary.

Finding the right person to make first contact with a prospect can be crucial and so it is worth spending a little time getting it right. Remember, this need not be the person who has been chosen to actually solicit a donation, but rather someone who knows the prospect and whom the prospect trusts and respects and who can then introduce the prospect to the asker.

First of all, make sure you have checked all your prospects against your Primary List (those prospects first identified by your governors and Senior Leadership Team). Then, if you have not done so already, check your database to see if you can ascertain who the prospect last had contact with at the school. Finally, show your ranked prospect list to your fundraising committee, if you have one, or to your alumni committee or parental association. As well as letting you know who they know amongst your prospect list, they may also be able to provide some useful intelligence about your prospects (if they have not done so already). At this point, you should be able to determine who is the best person to make initial contact with the prospect.

6.4 Conclusion

As I said in the introduction, major gift fundraising classically involves the following five stages:

1. Identification
2. Qualification
3. Cultivation
4. Solicitation
5. Stewardship

I have taken you through the first two stages of this process and you should now be in possession of a list of major gift prospects ready to be cultivated in support of your fundraising appeal. Or, at the very least, you know what you need to do to create such a list.

I have tried my best to take you step by step through the necessary stages in identifying and researching prospects, but there are some things that cannot be taught; they can only be learned through experience. With that in mind, I urge you to practise using the various resources and techniques described throughout the book.

Estimating someone's wealth and gift capacity is perhaps the hardest part of the whole process to get right – even for professionals – and so I suggest you practise using the various research resources (especially the Companies House websites) on one or two known millionaires. It is not hard to find them; just look in the

Sunday Times Rich List or one of the other rich lists which one can find on the internet. Don't go for the ultra-rich ones; their finances will take far too long to unravel. Rather pick someone low down the Rich List. Pick someone, in particular, who is described in the Rich List as owning a company. Look them up on one of the Companies House websites, paying particular attention to the turnover of the company, the net asset value, the profit or loss it is making. All of this will help you to see how they arrived at the value listed in the Sunday Times Rich List.

It is difficult to put into words the feelings of relief, satisfaction and, finally, pure joy you will feel when you first get a major gift from someone *you* have identified. It is something to be savoured. This will come, just as long as you remember to stay calm, stay methodical, and remember that Rome wasn't built in a day. Identifying and researching major gift prospects takes time, so take your time. Do it properly. And then you will reap the rewards.

Good luck to you!

Prospecting for Benefactors

Appendix A – Prospect spreadsheet

ID	Title	First name	Surname	Bank	Assets required?	Alumnus or parent?	On Primary List?
376	Mr	Douglas	Adams	HSBC Private Bank	£3m	Alumnus	Yes
158	Mr	William	Shakespeare	HSBC Private Bank	£3m	Alumnus	No
423	Mr	John	Tolkien	JP Morgan Private Bank	£3m	Alumnus	Yes
879	Mr	Herbert	Wells	Weatherbys Bank	£3m	Parent	No
355	Miss	Sophie	Hannah	Butterfield Bank	£1m	Alumnus	No
745	Mr	Ed	McBain	Butterfield Bank	£1m	Parent	No
634	Sir	Terence	Pratchett	Barclays Wealth	£500k	Alumnus	Yes
318	Mrs	Mary	Shelley	Arbuthnot Latham	£500k	Parent	No
364	Ms	Susanna	Clarke	Coutts & Co	£250k	Alumnus	No
542	Dr	Theo	Seuss	Coutts & Co	£250k	Alumnus	No

Appendix B – Private bank accounts

Bank	Assets Required
Adam & Co	£100k
Arbuthnot Latham	£500k
Bank of Scotland Private Banking	£250k assets, £100k salary
Banque Havilland	£1m
Barclays Wealth	£500k
BNP Paribas Wealth Management	£1m
Brown Shipley	£500k
Butterfield Bank	£1m
C Hoare & Co	£500k
Cater Allen Private Bank	£100k
Child & Co (RBS)	£100k
Citi Private Bank	£5m
Coutts & Co	£250k
Credit Suisse	£1m
Deutsche Bank	£250k
Drummonds Bank	£100k
Duncan Lawrie Private Banking	£250k
HSBC Private Bank	£3m
JP Morgan Private Bank	£3m
Julius Bär	£2m
Kleinwort Benson	£500k
Lloyds Private Banking	£250k assets, £100k salary
Lombard Odier	£5m
Morgan Stanley Private Bank	£2.5m
Natwest Private Banking	£100k assets, £100k salary
Nedbank Private Wealth	£275k assets, £80k salary
Pictet	£5m
Rathbone Brothers	£100k

Rothschild	£100k
Royal Bank of Canada	£500k
RBS Private Banking	£100k
SG Private Banking Hambros	£1m
Standard Chartered	£1m
UBS	£1m
Union Bancaire Privée	£500k
Weatherbys Bank	£3m assets, £300k salary

Appendix C – Qualification flow chart

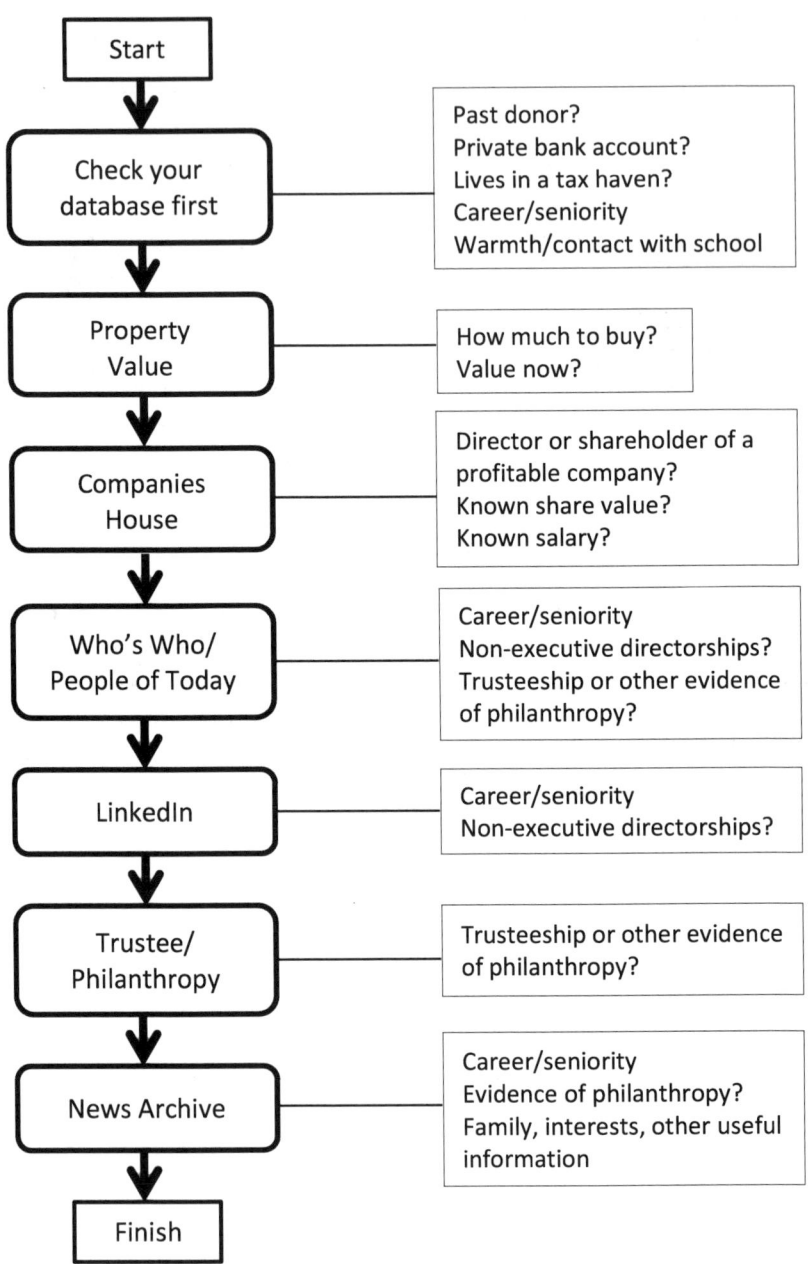

Appendix D – Ranked prospect list

Name	Gift Capacity	Warmth	Affinity	Total
Mr Douglas Adams	£100k	3	3	6
Mr Will Shakespeare	£100k	2	2	4
Mr John Tolkien	£75-£100k	3	3	6
Mr Herbert Wells	£75-£100k	3	1	4
Miss Sophie Hannah	£50-£75k	3	1	4
Mr Ed McBain	£50-£75k	2	2	4
Mr Roald Dahl	£50-£75k	2	1	3
Mr Charles Dickens	£50-£75k	1	1	2
Mr Neil Gaiman	£25-£50k	3	3	6
Mr Clive Lewis	£25-£50k	3	2	5
Mrs Mary Shelley	£25-£50k	2	1	3
Mr Jonathan Swift	£25-£50k	1	1	2
Ms Susanna Clarke	£25-£50k	1	1	2
Mr Ken Kesey	£10-£25k	3	2	5
Sir Terence Pratchett	£10-£25k	2	2	4
Dr Theophrastus Seuss	£10-£25k	1	2	3
Mr John Bunyan	£10-£25k	1	1	2
Mr Sebastian Faulks	£10-£25k	1	1	2

Acknowledgements.

I am very grateful to Michael Triff for his excellent comments on an earlier draft of this book and also for first introducing me to the world of the school development office.

I also wish to thank Felicity Rutland for giving me the opportunity of running a Development Office and Katherine Green for showing me how a school database ought to work.

Finally, I am very grateful to all the development staff, fundraisers and prospect researchers with whom I have worked over the years. Many of them have influenced the content of this book to some extent, but they bear no responsibility for its deficiencies.

I blame my parents for that.

Printed in Great Britain
by Amazon